BAD BEHAVIOR

Bad Behavior

Poems by Michael Steffen

BRICK ROAD
POETRY PRESS

Cover design: Keith Badowski

Author photo: Barbara Sullivan

Library of Congress Control Number: 2012952401
ISBN-13: 978-0-9835304-5-9

Published by Brick Road Poetry Press
P. O. Box 751
Columbus, GA 31902-0751
www.brickroadpoetrypress.com

Brick Road logo by Dwight New

I am deeply grateful to the late Eugene Monick for his thoughtful insights, to Jan Selving, April Ossmann, and Pam Bernard for their generous feedback and unflagging support, and to my teachers—Robin Behn, Nancy Eimers, Natasha Sajé, and Ralph Angel—for their kind and careful guidance.

CONTENTS

One

Two

Three

Four

I would have made a good Pope.

–Richard Nixon

One

Notes to My Obituarist

Mention my final minutes were spent
flirting with nurses and refusing narcotics.
Don't reveal that I loved knock-knock jokes,
or that I once filled in
for a saleswoman in lingerie
at Adam, Meldrum and Anderson's,
helping a few ladies find the right bra size,
mostly through a discerning glance,
never with a tape measure.
I'm giving you license to spice things up.

Tell the world I was born the day
Pius XII named Clare of Assisi
patron saint of television, that I was raised
in backward, benighted Buffalo,
an adventurer who lived longer than
I ever expected or deserved,

that the bulls of Pamplona ran from me,
that I skydived in three-piece suits,
scaled the Cliffs of Moher during an evening walk,
and died in a helicopter.
Say I am survived by my daughter, Emily,
my yet-to-be-born son, Diablo,

and my beloved spaniel, Scurvy. Tell the world
I was audacious, that my last words were *Watch This!*

A Working Act

Anyone who has ever hammered a nail up his nose owes a large debt to Melvin Burkhart.

—Todd Robbins, New York magician

He swore it didn't hurt.

Mimicking a Borscht Belt comic's droll patter,

he claimed he got his daily iron that way.

The nail penetrated the cavity

behind his right nostril, missing a dozen bone fragments,

his nose broken in a boxing match years before.

He worked in Ripley's Odditorium,

Ringling Brothers' and James E. Strait's

sideshows seven days a week,

thirty years onstage with Priscilla the Monkey Girl,

Lobster Boy, the Ossified Lady,

a man who boxed gorillas,

and three-eyed Bill Durkes (one fake, one intact, the third

a cleft palate above his nose).

A giant among snake wrestlers, stomach rotators,

survivors of the electric chair,

Melvin Burkhart could eat fire,

swallow swords,

breathe with one lung, tricks

left over from his early days as the Anatomical Man.
I watched him at the Sullivan Street Playhouse
suck in his stomach until I could see his backbone
and craned for a glimpse of the metal shank
stuck halfway into his head. *Step up, Son.*
See the Human Blockhead. He can do amazing things . . . .

Standing in a circle of people wincing
at what they'd paid to witness: the sound of steel tapping steel
and the spike's impossible disappearance
into his smiling, weathered face.

Killer

He still treats a piano like a drum.
Whole Lotta Shakin'
is a three-minute barrel roll,
F5 stomping its foot

above cocktail service clatter
pushing through
the whoop and holler of
Haney's Big House back in Ferriday.

Fifty years he's heard
Elvis this, Elvis that.
What the shit did Elvis do except
take dope I couldn't get a hold of?

Grey hair bounces to the beat.
How does he still grin
after six wives, two dead sons,
and the IRS dogging him since '79?

The Killer won't go quietly:

he kicks his stool out,
bangs the keys with elbows and fists,

sticks out his tongue, then sings

in a sour-mash, hillbilly drawl,

a pin-striped hip-shaker,

shuckin' and jivin'

just like the devil taught him.

New York

Three in the morning, I dance
the huckle-buck with my roomie—
two of us crooning
Some Enchanted Evening,
the hallway window open.

Mrs. Osadjca in 5D thinks
we're "homosectionals," thinks
in black and white, the flame
of Christian clarity. The light
beneath her locked door invites us
to serenade her

across a crowded room . . .
till we hear her cursing in Greek
while we fumble the wrong key
into our lock. The super's cat's
studied non-observance as we stagger

inside our floodlit apartment—
MINOLTA reds and greens
blazing through a shadeless pane—
a pigeon thumping its reflection,
radiator gargling,

my unset clock blinking

while I watch taxis trace

Manhattan—starless, moonless,

the din, the haze,

a working theory for night.

Nobody Gets In to See the Wizard

I'm checking my email and up pops this ad:
67% of women are unhappy
with the size of their lover's penis. Seems a
famous pharmacist has created *an herbal breakthrough*,
a revolutionary pill guaranteed to increase
circumference and dick length in a few short weeks.
My fingers hover above the keyboard.
I click on the link and wait
for the pledge of sexual prowess to cross my screen,
naked women throwing themselves at me.
Back in seventh grade, I deliberately
dropped my pencil beneath Mary Pasternak's
pristine desk, risking
discovery for a peek beneath
her school-issue skirt, her full mouth
auguring possibilities (*Great snatch*,
my pals agreed over lunch).
A Judy Garland look-alike,
pigtails, gingham, breasts I could
only dream of, though, once,
my weekly allowance bought me a glimpse
of Ruff Diamond's double Ds
at the county fair's sideshow striptease.
Blonde bouffant, spandex, heels—I watched,
awestruck, as she peeled

fabric from flawless skin and tossed

her white gloves at the whistling

dark—humongous,

untouchable. Her glance lifted me

above the catcalls, her body backlit with red light,

aurorean, the way, I mistakenly assumed,

lust would always look.

Every Woman's Friend

He's the one who never tells me
what he really wants.
He opens doors, pulls out chairs,
listens
to every word I say.
He understands I run late.
It's obvious to him
I have a life.
He dumped you? That ass!
Perhaps, he suggests,
Tom never loved you
the way *he* would—gently
admonishing me
should I imply it was my fault.
How could you think such a thing?
His shoulder is mine to cry on.
There, there . . . his fingers
tracing circles on my back.
And just for a second,
I wonder if his hand *slipped* down.
But the feeling passes
when he wipes away my tears.
Love ya',

he says, walking away.

And it sort of feels like

he does. Yeah.

To All Directors of Dead Teenager Movies

Why, in the beginning of your films,

do things always work as they should,

but after an hour, the laws of physics are suspended?

Vehicles that ran perfectly during the opening credits

fail to start as the slasher approaches.

A brand new flashlight, fresh from its package,

flickers for a second, then plunges

your snotty frat boy and bratty blonde bimbo

into darkness. Like any insomniac

channel-surfing at 3 am,

I'd like my terror less predictable.

Is it too much to ask that

your carload of pot-smoking adolescents

not take the shortcut down the creepy unpaved road?

I feel like I'm watching the same movie

over and over: strange noises in dark woods,

half-naked teens stumbling from brightly-lit

cabins. I see a person of color in your cast,

and I know their screen time is limited,

twenty minutes tops before they throw down

and shriek out a challenge to the lurking killer,

some brainless variation of *Come and get me!*

while standing in a pile of dead friends.

Forget the tropes of youngsters poking
their noses into places they don't belong,
or tracking shots from the lumbering
villain's point of view. I want to be surprised,
outsmarted. I want hell scared out of me.
I'm happiest when you frighten me half to death.
I promise I'll clutch a pillow to my face
and scream like a teen when the time comes.

Killing Time

When KRZ's top-forty fades,

I sing new words to an old song—

Poke her in the eye and skip to my Lou—

and my five-year-old instantly brightens.

Just trying to enliven the hours

and move us down the road.

She sings *Bop her on the head*

and skip to my Lou while we coast

through Binghamton's improvised hills,

our song getting grisly as we excise

fingernails, ears, kneecaps . . . .

I should set a better example,

but I've vaporized ants with glass,

shot crows off a wire with my .22.

There's no way I'm innocent.

By the time we hit Corning,

our victim is limbless. A bloated deer's

intestines curl on the shoulder

like cast-off ribbons. Organs litter the asphalt

from Scranton to the Nickel City.

Crazy

Her husband shot himself last spring,
but she saw him a few nights ago
sitting beside her on the flaking porch

telling her about the fields of Phu My,
about running through the charred grass,
shells exploding around him, how he knew

he was still alive, because he could hear
his dog tags clacking around his neck.
That evening, the widow's living room filled

with blood and shards: a twelve-point buck
crashed through the picture window
and thrashed, terrified, on her floor,

venetian blinds caught in his antlers.
She ran through the kitchen and held
the back door open, until

the delirious, bloody deer ran out.
The blinds trailed behind, then snagged
on her car's muffler.

She labored it free

then watched him run toward McMichael's Creek,

blinds still clacking in the branching bone.

Freefall

Skydivers jump, bellies earthward.

      Interlocking arms form a canopy.

   One loses his grip, plummets faster than his fellows,

      tugs his ripcord—

         nothing.

      His descent quickens. Too low to be helped,

  he can see parachutes blooming above him.

           Below,

a patchwork quilt grows larger;

    a highway centers itself in his path.

   He sheds excess weight—

 goggles, pack, his black boots rising

      through white wisps. To his left,

  a huge, blue reservoir. He aims for it,

    planing like a hawk toward the promise of fish,

but gravity claims him. In his last seconds,

  as he banks over small towns

      in verdant hills, he remembers

a poster he once tacked

to the back of his bedroom door—the *Swan Song* logo

of an angel falling through a backlit sky.

And here he is:

plunging from heaven, his eyes

saucered by the onrush, laughing

at this last inescapable twist

as the green earth widens to its final shape.

Lincoln Continental

In Henry Ford's Dearborn museum,
among fats and resins, antique furniture
and Oscar Mayer's Wienermobile, it sits
in front of a vintage McDonald's sign.

Trace your fingertip down the convertible's seat
where the President slumped into Jackie's arms.
You can almost feel the power

of its eight cylinders surging,
coil suspension absorbing shock,
rear leaf springs and live axle keeping
the suddenly swerving tires on the road.
Low, wide, and mighty,

the finest name ever to grace
a blood-soaked carpet, the shiny blue suicide doors.

Two

The Last Time Ajax Snapped His Collar

I tossed the bath sponge—fried in bacon grease,
squeezed to a marble-sized ball
and bound by twine—at his feet.

Whenever I stepped outside,
he strained his leash,
poised to tear out my throat.

How an animal becomes what he became
is no mystery. Lash and club—
I couldn't bear the yelps
his owner beat into silence.

He wasn't safe to live near,
but the rent was cheap.
The landlord's cruelty kept me
peering each night from behind the door
to see if the dog was chained.

There were nights I heard the landlord
beating his son, but once
he threatened to shoot his father
then turn the twelve-gauge on himself.

The cops took the boy away,

and when I heard Ajax choking

in the shadows, I had no regrets,

nor the next morning,

when I saw the landlord bent over

his bloated body, the unrolled tongue

still slick with drool as I squeezed past

and hurried down the walk.

News from Evergreen Commons

My mother is Bette Davis again,
elderly, roguish, eyes off-kilter,
v-shaped smile, a blaze
surrounding her no one dares touch.

She speaks with the same clipped bon mot.
You should neva say bad things
about the dead, you should only say good.
Joan Crawford is dead. Good.

In the cafeteria, we sit at a smoky table
while she fingers a cucumber sandwich
and glances outside at her Manhattan,
office towers lit, fur trotting beside fur.

She slips another Vantage from her clutch.
In the civil quiet between us, she notices
I'm reading Plath. *Ya know theya's a history*
of mental illness in ah famly.

Her mouth suddenly quivers
and her eyes brim. She slips off her black
skull cap, tosses her grey mane back.
Her lips are dark as blood.
We both know what is happening.

She is preparing to be lost forever,

and I: for the afternoon

we become completely polite.

How to Catch a Fly Ball with Your Teeth

Former employees of a local sawmill
kick their cleats against the dugout steps,
eager for practice.

Best to start with a Wiffle ball, advises the coach, *to develop technique.*
Then try a tennis ball. And finally, a baseball.
He doesn't recommend softballs:
their smooth covering makes it hard for teeth to grip.

The players listen intently.
Their empty sleeves dance in the wind.

Injury is minimal, Coach says, *if you follow a few basic guidelines.*
Always keep your eye on the ball.
Any miscalculation, and you could miss it completely.
It's all in the timing—

as the ball descends, you'll feel a brief moment of panic.
Breathe deep, Coach says,
and the players breathe.
Open your mouth as wide as possible.
They do.

Just before impact, you will feel a rush of air.
That's when you close your eyes.

Every Woman

Just a girl on your way to work,
brown hair, brown eyes, a hint
of lipstick on full lips,

I give you the inside seat, mumble
hello, and you light up with easy fire.
We chat, and I feel confident

until you snuggle against me.
Then I look for an empty seat
to escape to, but there is none.

You move closer, your arm in mine,
your heavy head leaning.
We kiss. This doesn't happen to me.

I'm the guy who sits alone on the bus,
goes home alone, eats alone, the guy who wants
what I've never had.

I give myself to you.
You are every fragrance that's ever existed,
every woman I've been terrified to know.

The Last Episode

Background to foreground, a blue-crested bird halts
in the middle of the road. Between two cliffs,
it stares at a mound of seed placed
on the striped macadam, then starts to peck.
An airy whistle, faint, then more insistent, sounds.
With a blink, the bird prepares to bolt.
A shadow falls as it flutters its tongue.
A solid *whump*, and a car-sized boulder plants itself
where the bird stood. The last impact tremor fades;
a moment of silence. The sun burns hot and high.
Rock formations tower above the desert floor,
purple shadows on scrub cactus. Crickets resume their chirring.

On a promontory above, the coyote lowers his binoculars.
No trail of dust leads from the scene,
just the boulder sitting in the road.
The coyote scampers down the ridge.
He inspects the elaborate mechanism he built,
where the catapult launched the stone from its sling.
His eyes follow the flight path down to the ground.
Beneath the boulder, a small trickle of blood.
The coyote's jaw drops. A smile crawls over his face.
His windy cough becomes a wheeze.

After several repetitions, it sounds like a laugh.

He dances wildly around the boulder,

howling at the sky. Finally!

No more mail-order rocket sleds, jet-powered pogo sticks,

do-it-yourself tornado kits, no more the denial of speed,

the avatar of rage and frustration . . . .

As the sun sets,

the coyote turns a spit above the fire outside his cave.

He listens to the crackling meat, driven half-mad by the aroma.

With the first bite, his eyes roll back, juice dribbles down his chin.

He lingers over each morsel, savors

the soft, chewy breast, the charred leg's crunch.

When he's licked the last grease drop, he lies back,

sated, stargazing, every mote of the creamy belt

cutting the sky in two. Cradled in the belly of the world,

the grand universe spread out before him,

he drifts into dreamless sleep. The credits roll.

Sympathy for the Devil

It still shellacs me—
Jagger's raunchy pout, his edge
of self-destruction, rebus of post-adolescent
fury, shrill caterwaul of truth
in the song's elegant disarray.
Tell me baby, what's my name.

In '68, the country was shocked, shamed.
First King, then Kennedy.
The only thing worth doing
was to fuck and acknowledge
our dual nature.

And so I did
with a girl whose name I've forgotten,
and while I did,
I heard the expanse of night,
an oblivion whirling around me,

unanswered secrets of the past
and a future roused by a ravenous force
hungry for war, disease, famine,
eager for someone to call forth
its dreadful power and feed.

PawnAmerica

While coins unravel in the metal scoop,

the farmer rakes with both hands, pushes four bits back

beneath the plastic. *A little something for your trouble*, watching

the silver backslide, the pewter crib shining like water,

fast-moving, deep. His coop was the first to go,

schoonered over by rain, prize pullets among the bloat.

Hogs bobbed like channel markers.

The teller counts a dozen twenties, a fistful of singles.

The farmer is mated now to a metal stamp, the memory

of bugs and stench. Wasn't it enough to suffer foreclosure,

each day parceled out by a shift whistle's moan?

Two forms of ID can't seem to slow this downward spiral,

or the roof-cracking river galloping toward him each night,

surging through the skull of his house, the runoff from fouled

bottomland where once his sluice glinted in twilight.

Snow Penis

Police arrested two boys last night
alleging they'd drawn with their feet,
on Parsipanny High School's front lawn,
a twenty-foot penis in snow (interesting,
how the cops felt compelled to measure it).

A harmless prank, just the sort of
dark humor we sometimes use
to cope with our lives and each other,

the simulation of crisis, a check on arrogance
or obliviousness, reminding us
not every newfound chest contains
precisely the treasure we'd expect.

Granted, such wisdom may not leap to mind
if, like me, you actually showed up
at a cross-dressing party your frat brothers claimed
would be held at a nearby sorority,

the door opened by a thunderstruck girl
covering her mouth with her hand
while you stood speechless in faux mink,
go-go boots and a beehive wig.

The Past

The way I loved the past
is the way I hate it now.
Always an underside,
some tearful departure resurrecting itself
every few years until death.

Maybe we all have some wrong in our lives
we just can't right, some sin
we can't outdistance, the rank smell of it
stalking us, bumming cigarettes,
wearing holes in its shoes.

On a Tour of Auburn State Prison

Four metal bolts anchor the chair
to grey basement floor.
Sitting in it, I imagine William Kemmler,
the first to die here.
He wears new brown trousers,
vest and spotless shirt. The scriptures are read.
He says *Amen* to everything.
Morning sun streams through a window
lighting his placid face. I see the monk's spot
shaved on the crown of his head
and the twenty-four faces surrounding him.
Now gentleman, the warden says,
looking at the witnesses,
This man killed Tillie Ziegler with a hatchet,
and I've told him he has got to die.
If he has anything to say, he'll say it now.
William looks up, composed,
recites in a thin, monotonous voice,
what he's committed to memory.
I wish everyone good luck in this world,
and I think I am going to a good place,
and the papers have been saying
a lot of stuff that isn't so. That's all I have to say.
Then he calmly adjusts his necktie,
sits down in the seat I'm sitting in now,

facing the seven terraced rows of benches.

The warden leans over,

drawing the straps tight around his arms.

It won't hurt, I promise.

The eyes that follow him are doglike, trusting,

but at times blank.

The warden fits the harness over William's face.

Straps cover his forehead, nose, most of his beard.

A group of doctors mills around, taking notes.

One wets the sponges of the two electrodes.

Another fits their cups to his head and spine.

Goodbye, says the warden.

Before William can respond, his body goes rigid

beneath the straining straps. The warden's watch

ticks seventeen seconds before he yells *Stop*.

William's forehead turns crudely dark,

his body frozen. A fly lights on his nose.

The witnesses draw near. *He's dead*, says one.

Oh yes, he's dead. But as they speak,

saliva drips from William's mouth.

His chest strains against the leather harness.

Turn on the current, the warden yells,

this man is not dead!

A sizzling, then billowing smoke—

two-thousand volts, long successive shocks,

arc down William's spine.

The room fills with the stench

of burning hair. He twitches again,

his body taut as piano wire. After thirty seconds,

they cut the current. Lights brighten.

The warden removes straps and harness.

Dark blood drips from William's ears.

His corpse, burned like a fuse,

retains its rigor, retains the chair's shape.

A hundred years finds me

listening to the chow horn blow,

the faint clink of leg irons, caged men stirring,

sitting on this same burnished wood.

Three

Ant Days

Swarming over it, blackening it,
breaking it into portable crumbs,

ruthlessly efficient,
ants carry off a discarded bun—

office ants on our cell phones,
holding ant board meetings

to balance our budgets,
army ants on peace-keeping missions,

carpenters devouring houses,
chef ants dreaming up menus,

and in the cafeteria serving
ant food, semi-digested; drones

at intercoms and security desks
monitoring ants like us,

red with effort or envy, pushing
no envelope, deplete, restore, deplete . . .

the great exhausted middle management
dropping from alcoholic bloat,

our ant bellies puffed, and migraines
from long ant days with short pay,

wondering how to keep
our large bucolic homes from ant foreclosure,

our tiny clogged hearts blowing open,
small black husks, each of us leaping

into the great ant abyss
in our hushed panic to feed.

Advice for a Famous Poet

I'm sick of reading your poems,
the ones where you stare for hours
at your neighbor's overgrown yard,
beech trees choking a Japanese maple
he really should cut down.
Stop looking out windows. It's clichéd.
No one has that kind of time.

Stop talking about Coltrane and Monk,
art cousining art. Start fresh.
It's the twenty-first century:
stop using *hi-fi* in your poems,
quit telling us about typewriters
you haven't used in thirty years,
your Underwood's lacquer-cracked keys.

Stop describing
every meal you've eaten. Ditto the cat
lounging on your davenport.
Enough with that damp English drizzle.

I know you've been around the block.
You think you know something about love
and its dark derangements, but you don't,

so spare me that bullshit image

of leaves clinging to a dying branch.

Business Trip

His wife made love to him
with customary affection
at the end of his last day
without shame.

He felt nothing
when his best friend lay beneath him,
grafted to his rise and fall,
her sighs feathering his hair,

except for the moment
she dug a nail into his skin,
a needle in his chest he thought was love.

Lucifer's Wife

You could talk Lazarus back to his grave.
If deceit is your business, pleasure is your art.

I expected you to appear
as a dark tornado's eye,

a vulture, perhaps—scraps of flesh
hanging from your hooked beak.

You came to me first
as the burning sword of morning,

and it would be a lie to say
I did not crave

your inhuman lust, nor rise up in flames
as we kissed, parted. You whispered

your scalding light
into the flushed curve of my ear, dark dreams.

Getting up in the Morning

Your bathrobe waits to wrap you in its arms,
walk you downstairs, pour some coffee.

Fence-jumping sheep you counted last night
back into their somnambulant pen.
Sun claims your window.

You dismiss the covers
and lift from the pillow your groggy head
trying to retain an image,
a vaguely familiar woman
about to answer your most urgent question—gone,

even while your bed leans on its oars
eager to ferry you back to sleep.

A Little Murder

We are re-empowering you, proactively
repositioning you outside the company,
which is where we like to allocate any
excess of our requirements, a win-win.
Nothing to do with your age or health.
For business reasons, we've decruited
certain operational reserves, what we call
dynamic resource cessation. Fear not
our indubitable Kevorking of redundancy,
a constructive, highly positive
separation, if you will,
of your skills from ours.

She Made Toothpicks of the Timber of My Heart

The stereo is tuned to a country station
in the open-windowed house next door—
something about his heart, a diamond,
her clubbing him with a spade—cranked so loud
I can hear the scraping of high heels
as a woman leaves a man, some line about
his soul stomped flat.

When my neighbor's lonesome winds blow,
I hear someone doing hard time in Folsom,
a train coming 'round a bend, because
there's always a train coming.

That's what this tune is for—
cutting through the godforsaken
silence, solitude, despair . . . .

Spin Cycle

First it's lilies, then roses,

black limo, white limo, chicken or fish . . . .

For two hours, you tell me

how you can't get anything done,

how sick you feel, how miserable life is.

When I ask, *Honey,*

is there something I can do? you tell me

I'm not listening, not being

supportive, what you need

is someone to help you figure out how

to do everything

yourself, but I suspect

you're overwhelmed

when you should be happy,

and no objective, no matter how principled,

is worth this litany

of rancor, tears. All I want

is to relieve your burden, and you say,

If that helps you, *fine, go ahead,*

but it doesn't do a fucking thing for me.

Now I'm caught in the spin—

ocularis infernum, swirling wind and flame

sucking me into its maelstrom—

you catch me rolling my eyes,

and there I go again:

your needs are not being met,

and *Maybe*, you say,

I should just shower and

get fitted for the goddamn dress

and go sleep in a park somewhere.

You storm out,

and my insensitive self is left

listening to this incredible buzzing in his ears,

thinking of lilies in a crystal bowl

and how long they can float in water,

surrounded by candles, before they start to sink.

Ars Dyslexia

Words travel down my arm
and disappear.
My eyes go different.
Something else comes out of my pen.
When I spell a sound,
letters leapfrog.

Sometimes an error works—
I took my god for a walk,
stroked his warm muzzle, or
the only sure things in life
are death and texas.

Writing a poem is like
driving in a foreign country—
steering on the opposite side,
and all the time moving faster
in the wrong direction.

The Rag Wars

Within feet of my unsuspecting head,
she hurled her sopping arsenal—
my sister pasting me with oil soap.
Mopping wet, I fired back,
hoping to best her with speed
and a balled-up tee-shirt. Hours
she defended the furnace and workbench,
while I held the laundry room, flinching
each time she walloped me
with frayed scraps of Mother's bathrobe
torn by my father when he sprawled
in the driveway, beer-soaked
flannel she'd ripped from his shoulders
trying to drag him into the house.
Coughing, spluttering,
half-blinded by detergent,
I copied the way he wind-milled,
while my sister flashed our mother's anger,
slapped stoned cotton across my cheek,
strafed me over and over,
reddening my face. And again
as I howled, her wet towel snapping,
the sting of her laughter.

Industry

After a blizzard, children in snowsuits
and knitted hats sled down
the cindered slope of Columbus Avenue
behind a plow truck angling speckled snow
into the driveways of bowed houses.
They shout across the widening street,
the morning punctuated by their shrieks.
Two young men—they must be brothers—
lean on my doorbell, a gloveless pair in do-rags,
their sweatshirts stained and frayed,
balancing shovels across bony shoulders—
eighteen, maybe twenty. I've noticed them
odd-jobbing around the neighborhood,
burning leaves last fall, washing windows,
hauling trash . . . . They're back
in sweats and unlaced sneakers offering
to clear my drive—forty feet, ten bucks each.
I grew up in Buffalo, climbed coal fields behind
Bethlehem Steel with my two best friends, stared
at a dense carpet of stinking algae
floating near the lake's edge, the shoreline
crammed with docks, cement slabs, steel cribs.
I sat on the warming coal with Tim and Tommy—
a late spring wind kicking up dust,

filling our eyes with tears.

Tommy dropped out of Seneca Vocational,

worst school in Western New York,

and Tim blended into Lackawanna Juvenile

with other boys destined to be men

without futures, money, or the prospect of it—

stoop-shouldered brothers who hauled

hammers and saws from house to house,

cut grass, washed and waxed for cash,

did what was needed then walked home,

rank and filthy and callused,

rubbing their leathery palms together.

I hand them each a ten.

"First Things First"

No wonder our parents were so intent
on teaching us what to do when
the phone's ringing, someone's at the door,
our hand is on a hot stove,
and we need to go to the bathroom—
to be absolutely certain, as adults,
in that baffling shuffle of choices,
where to begin, and why.

You'd think it would be obvious
in the echelon of things to do,
but someone at some point
dragged a cart from a barn
and placed his horse behind it—
the earliest failure of common sense—
man and beast standing in rain,
puzzling over their lack of movement.

Four

Adios, Sweet Larry

*The most traumatic part for his family was getting him into the
coffin—they put his left leg in, and then the trouble started.*

—Obituary on the death of Larry LaPrise,
author of *The Hokey Pokey*

I remember huge circles peopled

by mothers, fathers, uncles, aunts,

mouthing the chorus, my big-breasted

grandmother bouncing in her flowered dress—

all that wonderful fat jiggling—her hands

on her hips, wheezing, *Oh Jesus*

as we shook our butts and twirled.

Someone told me the lyrics

were derived from the Catholic Mass,

which I find a stretch to believe—a distortion

of *hoc enim est corpus meum, this is my body,*

words of consecration elevating the host—

though, after eight beers at a wedding,

I'm sure I could be convinced.

Adios, Sweet Larry.

You put your whole self in,

you took your whole self out.

Ghost Wedding

We are somewhere in the bowels
of Penn Station, surrounded by
Smoothie King, McDonald's,
Hot n' Crusty Cinnamon Buns.
Commuters bustle, doors slam,
a train inches from the station.

The Lake Shore Limited
edges past a minister shifting
from foot to shoeless foot,
his torn black raincoat
buttoned up to his neck.
A decision has to be made.

Our future rides the blue-flecked
rail and vanishes in the dark
tunnel. You cradle a bloody fetus,
humming it to sleep. Its tiny fists clench
and unclench. The noise is deafening.

Bypass

I have a taste for back-alley sex,
whisk of a snare, the alto's raspy bark,
bock beer in a glass mug,
anything maroon, torpid and ruthless.

But I have a scar on my chest,
a mottled, burning crescent,
slim corridor raised, my days stitched
across its surface, brief ribbon.

I still wander from bar to bar on Houston,
blue smoke and velvet, mist
sizzling on blacktop, though now I just watch
those beautiful, shirtless, rough-trade boys.

Mirror

She stood motionless at the stove,
    staring at a pot of potatoes
        boiling over.

I was sick with measles, my room
    at the end of a dark hallway,
        and watched through my open door

as she turned, leaned against the oven,
    and slid a hand over her bald head.
        She slowly opened her robe and traced

a trail of stitches across her chest—
    skin pitted and sliced—a jagged red line
        disappearing beneath her armpit.

For the first time, I could see
    my mother's left breast was gone.
        It was hot—

the place on my chest
    where I could not stop my hand from going,
        trying to soothe her, cover her up.

Synonymy

I discover, while dragging my unabridged finger
through Roget's *S's*,
that *synonym*, itself, has no synonym,

presenting me with an ironic leap
from *synergy* to *synopsis*.

                        Now and then,
I like to see what's up with this world—
what's related, what's not;

I like otherness, how *verse* is a different name
for *poem*, how writing a poem is like naming
an unborn child, how words cling to each other—

nude writhing with *naked*,
sycophant following *brownnose* around,
nothing, nada, and *zilch*

passing between them their torch of absence—
and how the right word finally frees itself
from the many wedged beside it,

staring into the white shallows,

diving off the tip of my tongue,

parsing air.

Honeymoon

I remember your skin's lit sheen,

your body cradled in moonlight, the evening

I watched you shuddering, inconsolable

because I'd yelled, *What's your excuse this time?*

my body wanting to feel

the pleasure you could not,

as if frustration over those countless nights

was mine alone. I said, knowing even then

whatever words I spoke would fail,

each phrase one step further

from the pleasure I sought, *I'm sorry, I love you,*

but you cried, *Who cares?* lifted your arm,

covered your eyes and turned

your freckled back to me. I traced the curve

of your hip beneath the coverlet,

pressed against you, but you didn't respond.

I paid for my words and sat, miles away,

on the edge of the bed. All night cicadas hummed

a throbbing song that died in slow degrees.

Happiness

March sun thaws my stiff coat,
a frozen tear on my cheek,

revealing its warmth so slowly
you'd swear nothing changed at all.

It's been a while since I've revealed
what I feel.

I've made excuses,
constructed evasions, been harsh,

or said nothing—
my greatest regret.

You know how some people say
one moment of clarity is enough

to understand everything?
This morning, in the back woods,

I saw sun break through the trees.
On snow-laden, wet moss, I felt an old love,

rocks and ferns and pine boughs,

a soft glow in the hemlocks.

At the Fertility Clinic

He must do it standing in a three-by-four foot booth,
Furious Facials unspooling in the VCR.
Badly lit—

the women he will give this moment to—
Chrissy Shakes, C.C. Rider, Vanessa Del Rio . . .
his sudden flush, glimpsing

white test tubes stacked in a half-opened freezer.
Spermsicles, the technician jokes.
Sometimes I feel like a Madam.

She hands him a beaker, baby wipes. *Be sure
to wash your hands. Don't touch
the insides of the cup.* What it's come to—

snake charmers coaxing him erect,
girls with marcelled hair, high heels,
thongs. It takes engineering now,

a little *Cream of the Crop*—the hypnotic
stroking, a whisper in his ear—*Baby,
you know you want this*—more

like a question flickering

around him, a tightening collar.

Yes, Baby, yes.

The Seduction of Lot

It reads like a porno script—

    Genesis 19:30-35.

        Thinking they were alone on earth,

and to save his bloodline,

    Lot's daughters offered him wine,

        sprawled him

in their cavern's feathered gloom.

    He was drunk when he slept with them,

        but I think he knew

what God had burned in his heart

    must be fulfilled,

        that all children are the seeds of God,

even the children of the children of Lot.

    He knew each daughter when she lay down

    and when she rose.

The eldest bore him a son,

    as did the younger.

        I think Lot was afraid—

not when the Lord rained fire on Sodom,

    nor when his fleeing wife

        in the instant she looked back

fused to that moment—

    but only when he entered his daughters,

        frightened by the power of his lust,

then his shame

    as he watched, over time,

        their bellies swelling to preserve his seed.

Goatism

It begins with Aristotle,

who argues that a statement is either right,

or it's not. There's no middle ground.

                                        He can't say

Nothing is a goat. He's seen them

munching tufts on rocky cliffs above Athens.

The opposite must be true.

Now there are goats everywhere—

chasing cars, swimming upstream, performing

appendectomies, goats

who make themselves small, fit into cat suits,

invisible, faster-than-light goats.

Birds, doors, numbers, pencils—

there's nothing a goat can't be.

Never has a species so proliferated.

Extend Aristotle's argument to parts of goats,

and you'll find no difference between

a goat and its leg. Extend it further,

and you'll have the "All-goat," a fusion of

actual and potential goats, a rather exceptional goat in view of its numerous horns and tails.

The "All-goat" has many heads.

Insomnia

Turn down your blanket.

Climb inside,

pillow on pillow, crisp clean sheets.

Here is muscular slumber.

Night is a long road,

lightning a filament,

one nerve in a mica lamp.

Let the drumming rain erase you.

Watching My Mother Sleep

The morphine she's been given for the pain
in her shattered hip kicks in. She rocks back
and forth beneath a thin hospital sheet,
slowly stretches her arms heavenward
until I ease them down. All night

her restless hands reach toward something,
someone I can't see—
relief, an invisible embrace . . . .
I wish she'd tell me what she wants.
Her fingers point to every possible desire.

The Hermit Crab

How did it get there,
the dark circular shell, no larger than a penny,
just beyond my deckchair
on the white tile bordering the pool?

Wait staff hurried around the perimeter,
balancing trays of exotic cocktails,
handing towels to guests.
Amid the occasional splash and flurry
of sandaled feet, the small shell crept.

Certain it would be swept away
by the pool's overflow, crushed underfoot,
or scooped, perhaps, into a palm and tossed,
I watched it creep along, mesmerized,
strangely bound by the rules of chance.

The crab reached the pool's edge.
Just ahead, a waterfall spilled over
a tiled ledge. I cringed as it threatened
to overwhelm the creature
with a sudden onrush, wash it in.

The crab continued crawling,
climbing, trying to climb. I held my breath
while each averted hazard
recorded its wandering path:

a busboy mopping, the spreading slick
from a knocked-over bottle of Coppertone,
near the oblivious couple
sitting on the tiled edge, their legs
dangling in water, and beyond
my craning neck, my vanishing line of sight.

What struck me then was not
all the dangers I could predict,
nor the depth of my resolve
not to interfere with its destiny,
but the oddly persistent feeling that

this intrepid creature, beacon of tenacity,
unaware of its own tenuous survival,
of the perils that menaced it on all sides,
clung to fate's fraying rope
and kept moving forward, inch by
unsteady inch, *despite* the unforeseeable
closing in from everywhere.

Notes

A Working Act. This poem was inspired by a profile of Melvin Burkhart which aired on National Public Radio's "All Things Considered" on November 13th, 2001.

The Last Episode. Inspiration for this poem came from *The Unauthorized Biography of Wile E. Coyote* by Cheeseburger Brown.

PawnAmerica. The actual name of a pawnbroker's shop in Allentown, Pennsylvania.

On a Tour of Auburn State Prison. William Kemmler was the first person to die in the electric chair. He was executed at Auburn State Prison on August 6th, 1890.

She Made Toothpicks of the Timber of My Heart. A country-western song authored by Dick Sanford and Sammy Mysels.

Ars Dyslexia. Credit goes to comedian Bix Brillo for the line about "death and texas."

Goatism. This poem is partly derived from the now-defunct website, www.goatism.org.

Acknowledgments

Grateful acknowledgment is made to the editors of the following publications in which some of these poems first appeared, occasionally in slightly different forms:

"Adios, Sweet Larry," *The Night Bomb Review*

"Advice for a Famous Poet" appeared in *Smartish Place* as "How to Write a Poem."

"Ars Dyslexia" appeared in *Bloodroot* as "Dyslexic."

"Every Woman's Friend," *Straylight*

"Freefall" and "Notes to My Obituarist," *Third Wednesday*

"Happiness" appeared in *Into the Teeth of the Wind* as "Dearly Beloved."

"Honeymoon" appeared in *Into the Teeth of the Wind* as "Planets Still Crave Their Suns Over Impossible Distances."

"Killer" appeared in *Broken Plate* as "Jerry Lee Lewis."

"Mirror" appeared in *Fox Chase Review* as "Mirror-Touch."

"New York," *Nidus* and *Schuylkill Valley Journal of the Arts*

"News from Evergreen Commons," *Fox Chase Review*

"Nobody Gets In to See the Wizard," *The Ledge*

"On a Tour of Auburn State Prison," *E Pluribus Unum: An Anthology of Diverse Voices*

"PawnAmerica," *Comstock Review*

"Spin Cycle" appeared in *Birmingham Poetry Review* as "The Spin."

"The Past," *Verdad*

"The Seduction of Lot," *Italian American Writers.com*

About the Author

Michael Steffen is the author of two previous poetry collections—*No Good at Sea* (Legible Press, 2002) and *Heart Murmur* (Bordighera Press, 2009). His poems have appeared in a wide variety of journals including *Poetry*, *Potomac Review*, *The Ledge*, *Poet Lore*, *Rhino*, and many others. In 2002, Michael was granted a Fellowship from the Pennsylvania Council on the Arts. He is a Y2K graduate of the MFA in Creative Writing Program at Vermont College and currently lives in Lancaster, NY.

Our Mission

The mission of Brick Road Poetry Press is to publish and promote poetry that entertains, amuses, edifies, and surprises a wide audience of appreciative readers. We are not qualified to judge who deserves to be published, so we concentrate on publishing what we enjoy. Our preference is for poetry geared toward dramatizing the human experience in a language rich with sensory image and metaphor, recognizing that poetry can be, at one and the same time, both familiar as the perspiration of daily labor and outrageous as a carnival sideshow.

BRICK ROAD
POETRY PRESS

Also Available from Brick Road Poetry Press

www.brickroadpoetrypress.com

Dancing on the Rim by Clela Reed

Possible Crocodiles by Barry Marks

Pain Diary by Joseph D. Reich

Otherness by M. Ayodele Heath

Drunken Robins by David Oates

Damnatio Memoriae by Michael Meyerhofer

Lotus Buffet by Rupert Fike

The Melancholy MBA by Richard Donnelly

Two-Star General by Grey Held

Chosen by Toni Thomas

Etch and Blur by Jamie Thomas

Water-Rites by Ann E. Michael

About the Prize

The Brick Road Poetry Prize, established in 2010, is awarded annually for the best book-length poetry manuscript. Entries are accepted August 1st through November 1st. The winner receives $1000 and publication. For details on our preferences and the complete submission guidelines, please visit our website at www.brickroadpoetrypress.com.

Made in the USA
Charleston, SC
12 December 2012